A
GATHERING
OF
ANGELS

Edited by Jill Wolf

Paintings courtesy of Superstock

ISBN 0-89954-448-7

CONTENTS

Do not forget to entertain strangers, for by so doing some people have entertained angels without knowing it.

Hebrews 13:2 (NIV)

The guardian angels of life sometimes fly so high as to be beyond our sight, but they are always looking down upon us.

—Jean Paul Richter

Bearers of Glad Tidings   29

The angel answered, "I am Gabriel. I stand in the presence of God, and I have been sent to speak to you and to tell you this good news."

Luke 1:19 (NIV)

Dark Angels   39

All God's angels come to us disguised . . .

—*James Russell Lowell*

ENTERTAINING ANGELS

Do not forget to entertain strangers, for by so doing some people have entertained angels without knowing it.

Hebrews 13:2 (NIV)

I throw my selfe down in my Chamber, and I call in and invite God, and His Angels thither . . .

—*John Donne*

. . . every religion, every scripture, asserts the fact of the existence of Angels and of their occasional appearances among men.

—*Annie Besant*

The angels keep their ancient places;— Turn but a stone, and start a wing!

—*Francis Thompson*

Outside the open window The morning air is all awash with angels.

—*Richard Wilbur*

Angels at the Creation

"Where were you when I laid the earth's foundation? Tell me, if you understand. Who marked off its dimensions? Surely you know! Who stretched a measuring line across it? On what were its footings set, or who laid its cornerstone—while the morning stars sang together and all the angels shouted for joy?"

Job 38:4-7 (NIV)

Jacob's Ladder

Jacob left Beersheba and set out
for Haran. When he reached a
certain place, he stopped for the
night because the sun had set.
Taking one of the stones there, he
put it under his head and lay down
to sleep. He had a dream in which
he saw a stairway resting on the
earth, with its top reaching to
heaven, and the angels of God
were ascending and descending
on it.

Genesis 28:10-12 (NIV)

Jacob Wrestles the Angel

So Jacob was left alone, and a man wrestled with him till daybreak. When the man saw that he could not overpower him, he touched the socket of Jacob's hip so that his hip was wrenched as he wrestled with the man. Then the man said, "Let me go, for it is daybreak."

But Jacob replied, "I will not let you go unless you bless me."

The man asked him, "What is your name?"

"Jacob," he answered.

Then the man said, "Your name will no longer be Jacob, but Israel, because you have struggled with God and with men and have overcome."

Genesis 32:24-28 (NIV)

He struggled with the angel and overcame him; he wept and begged for his favor.

Hosea 12:4 (NIV)

Choir of Angels
Master of the Life of the Virgin

The Celestial Hierarchy

A traditional hierarchy of angels, ranked from highest to lowest into nine orders or choirs, according to the writings of Dionysius and St. Thomas Aquinas

The First Hierarchy
(those closest to God who contemplate God's goodness)

Seraphim

Cherubim

Thrones

The Second Hierarchy
(those who preside over the ordering of the universe)

Dominions

Virtues

Powers

The Third Hierarchy
(those who direct the ordering of human affairs)

Principalities

Archangels

Angels

Reflections of Light

Angels are intelligent reflections of light,
that original light which has no beginning.
They can illuminate. They do not need
tongues or ears, for they can communicate
without speech, in thought . . . They are
limited in their powers: when in Heaven
they cannot be on earth at the same time,
and when God sends them to earth, they
cannot remain in Heaven at the same time.
Yet they are not captive to walls and
doors; in this respect they are unlimited.
When God sends them to appear to good
men, they do not reveal themselves in their
true shape, but in a changed semblance
that men can see . . . As disembodied
mind, they live in a mental climate and are
not limited as bodies are. They do not
need the three dimensions. Wherever they
are sent, they are there as mind and there
can take on power, but they cannot do this
in more than one place at a time.

—John of Damascus

An angel is an intelligent essence, always in motion. It has free will, is incorporeal, serves God, and has been bestowed with immortality.

—John of Damascus

It is not because angels are holier than men or devils that makes them angels, but because they do not expect holiness from one another, but from God alone.

—William Blake

An angel can illuminate the thought and mind of man by strengthening the power of vision . . .

—St. Thomas Aquinas

If . . . we would cast the gift of a lovely thought into the heart of a friend, that would be giving as the angels give.

—George Macdonald

I want to be an angel
And with the angels stand,
A crown upon my forehead,
A harp within my hand.

—*Urania Locke Bailey*

I love to hear the story
Which angel voices tell.

—*Emily Miller*

"Angel" is the only word in the language which can never be worn out.

—*Victor Hugo*

Music is well said to be the speech of angels.

—*Thomas Carlyle*

"Good night, sweet prince: and flights of angels sing thee to thy rest."

—*William Shakespeare*

Angel with Violin
Fra Angelico, c. 1387-1455, Italian

GUARDIAN ANGELS

"See, I am sending an angel ahead of you to guard you along the way and to bring you to the place I have prepared. Pay attention to him and listen to what he says."

Exodus 23:20,21 (NIV)

If you make the Most High your dwelling . . . then no harm will befall you, no disaster will come near your tent. For He will command His angels concerning you to guard you in all your ways; they will lift you up in their hands, so that you will not strike your foot against a stone.

Psalm 91:9-12 (NIV)

. . . God that loves His creatures so . . .
That blessèd angels He sends to and fro . . .

—Edmund Spenser

The guardian angels of life sometimes fly
so high as to be beyond our sight, but they
are always looking down upon us.

—Jean Paul Richter

A guardian angel o'er his life presiding,
Doubling his pleasures, and his cares
    dividing.

—Samuel Rogers

God, which dwelleth in heaven, prosper
your journey, and the angel of God keep
you company.

—The Apocrypha

Angel of God, my Guardian dear,
To whom God's love entrusts me here;
Ever this day be at my side,
To light and guard,
To rule and guide.

—Traditional Prayer

Four angels to my bed.
Four angels round my head,
One to watch and one to pray,
And two to bear my soul away.

—Thomas Ady

Hail, Guardian Angels of the House!
Come to our aid,
Share with us our work and play.
Be with us that we may hear your wings,
And feel your breath upon our cheek . . .

—Geoffrey Hodson

Music-Making Angel with Violin
Melozzo da Forli, 1438-1494, Italian
The Vatican Museums & Galleries, Rome

After He drove the man out, He placed
on the east side of the Garden of Eden
cherubim and a flaming sword flashing
back and forth to guard the way to the
tree of life.

Genesis 3:24 (NIV)

√   With the coming of dawn, the angels
urged Lot, saying, "Hurry! Take your
wife and your two daughters who are
here, or you will be swept away when
the city is punished."

When he hesitated, the men grasped
his hand and the hands of his wife and
of his two daughters and led them
safely out of the city, for the Lord was
merciful to them.

Genesis 19:15,16 (NIV)

An Angel Saves Isaac

When they reached the place God had told him about, Abraham built an altar there and arranged the wood on it. He bound his son Isaac and laid him on the altar, on top of the wood. Then he reached out his hand and took the knife to slay his son. But the angel of the Lord called out to him from heaven, "Abraham! Abraham!"

"Here I am," he replied.

"Do not lay a hand on the boy," he said. "Do not do anything to him."

Genesis 22:9-12 (NIV)

Balaam and the Angel

Then the Lord opened Balaam's eyes, and he saw the angel of the Lord standing in the road with his sword drawn. So he bowed low and fell facedown.

The angel of the Lord asked him, "Why have you beaten your donkey these three times? I have come here to oppose you because your path is a reckless one before me. The donkey saw me and turned away from me these three times. If she had not turned away, I would certainly have killed you by now, but I would have spared her."

Balaam said to the angel of the Lord, "I have sinned. I did not realize you were standing in the road to oppose me. Now if you are displeased, I will go back."

Numbers 22:31-34 (NIV)

An Angel Warns Joseph

When they had gone, an angel of the Lord appeared to Joseph in a dream. "Get up," he said, "take the child and His mother and escape to Egypt. Stay there until I tell you, for Herod is going to search for the child to kill Him."

So he got up, took the child and His mother during the night and left for Egypt, where he stayed until the death of Herod.

Matthew 2:13-15 (NIV)

After Herod died, an angel of the Lord appeared in a dream to Joseph in Egypt and said, "Get up, take the child and His mother and go to the land of Israel, for those who were trying to take the child's life are dead."

So he got up, took the child and His mother and went to the land of Israel.

Matthew 2:19-21 (NIV)

Angels Attend Jesus

Again, the devil took Him to a very high mountain and showed Him all the kingdoms of the world and their splendor. "All this I will give You," he said, "if You will bow down and worship me."

Jesus said to him, "Away from Me, Satan! For it is written: 'Worship the Lord your God, and serve Him only.'"

Then the devil left him, and angels came and attended Him.

Matthew 4:8-11 (NIV)

Angel with Lute
Rosso Florentino
15th Century, Italian

"See that you do not look down
on one of these little ones. For I
tell you that their angels in heaven
always see the face of My Father
in heaven."

Matthew 18:10,11 (NIV)

Where Shall the Baby's Dimple Be?

Over the cradle a mother hung,
Softly crooning a slumber song;
And these were the simple words
   she sung
All the evening long:

"Cheek or chin, or knuckle or knee,
Where shall the baby's dimple be?
Where shall the angel's finger rest
When he comes down to the
   baby's nest?
Where shall the angel's touch remain
When he awakens my babe again?"

Still as she bent and sang so low,
A murmur into her music broke;
And she paused to hear, for she
   could but know
The baby's angel spoke.

"Cheek or chin, or knuckle or knee,
Where shall the baby's dimple be?
Where shall my finger fall and rest
When I come down to the baby's nest?
Where shall my finger's touch remain
When I awaken your babe again?"

Silent the mother sat, and dwelt
Long in the sweet delay of choice;
And then by her baby's side she knelt,
And sang with pleasant voice:

"Not on the limb, O angel dear!
For the charm with its youth
    will disappear;
Not on the cheek shall the dimple be,
For the harboring smile will fade and flee;
But touch thou the chin with
    an impress deep,
And my baby the angel's seal shall keep."

—*Josiah G. Holland*

The angels all were singing out of tune,
And hoarse with having little else to do,
Excepting to wind up the sun and moon,
Or curb a runaway young star or two.

—*Lord Byron*

Bearers of Glad Tidings

Zechariah and Gabriel √

Then an angel of the Lord appeared to him, standing at the right side of the altar of incense. When Zechariah saw him, he was startled and was gripped with fear. But the angel said to him: "Do not be afraid, Zechariah; your prayer has been heard. Your wife Elizabeth will bear you a son, and you are to give him the name John. He will be a joy and delight to you, and many will rejoice because of his birth, for he will be great in the sight of the Lord."

Luke 1:11-15 (NIV)

∨

Zechariah asked the angel, "How can I be sure of this? I am an old man and my wife is well along in years."

The angel answered, "I am Gabriel. I stand in the presence of God, and I have been sent to speak to you and to tell you this good news. And now you will be silent and not able to speak until the day this happens, because you did not believe my words, which will come true at their proper time."

Luke 1:18-20 (NIV)

The Annunciation

In the sixth month, God sent the angel Gabriel to Nazareth, a town in Galilee, to a virgin pledged to be married to a man named Joseph, a descendant of David. The virgin's name was Mary. The angel went to her and said, "Greetings, you who are highly favored! The Lord is with you."

Mary was greatly troubled at his words and wondered what kind of greeting this might be. But the angel said to her, "Do not be afraid, Mary, you have found favor with God. You will be with child and give birth to a son, and you are to give Him the name Jesus. He will be great and will be called the Son of the Most High."

Luke 1:26-32 (NIV)

Angels at the Annunciation   1469-1543, Italian
Francesco Granacci   Galleria dell'Academia, Florence

The Angel Speaks to Joseph

. . . Mary was pledged to be married to Joseph, but before they came together, she was found to be with child through the Holy Spirit. Because Joseph her husband was a righteous man and did not want to expose her to public disgrace, he had in mind to divorce her quietly.

But after he had considered this, an angel of the Lord appeared to him in a dream and said, "Joseph son of David, do not be afraid to take Mary home as your wife, because what is conceived in her is from the Holy Spirit."

Matthew 1:18-20 (NIV)

The Shepherds and the Angels

And there were shepherds living out in the fields nearby, keeping watch over their flocks at night. An angel of the Lord appeared to them, and the glory of the Lord shone around them, and they were terrified. But the angel said to them, "Do not be afraid. I bring you good news of great joy that will be for all the people. Today in the town of David a Savior has been born to you; He is Christ the Lord. This will be a sign to you: You will find a baby wrapped in cloths and lying in a manger."

Suddenly a great company of the heavenly host appeared with the angel, praising God and saying, "Glory to God in the highest, and on earth peace to men on whom His favor rests."

Luke 2:8-14 (NIV)

It Came Upon the Midnight Clear

It came upon the midnight clear,
That glorious song of old,
From angels bending near the earth,
To touch their harps of gold:
"Peace on the earth, good-will to men,
From heaven's all gracious King:"
The world in solemn stillness lay
To hear the angels sing.

Still through the cloven skies
    they come,
With peaceful wings unfurled;
And still their heavenly music floats
O'er all the weary world:
Above its sad and lowly plains
They bend on hovering wing,
And ever o'er its Babel sounds
The blessed angels sing.

—Edmund H. Sears

Hark! the Herald Angels Sing

Hark! the herald angels sing,
"Glory to the new-born King;
Peace on earth, and mercy mild,
God and sinners reconciled!"
Joyful all ye nations rise,
Join the triumph of the skies;
With th' angelic host proclaim,
"Christ is born in Bethlehem."
Hark! the herald angels sing,
"Glory to the new-born King."

—Charles Wesley

The Resurrection

After the Sabbath, at dawn on the first day of the week, Mary Magdalene and the other Mary went to look at the tomb.

There was a violent earthquake, for an angel of the Lord came down from heaven and, going to the tomb, rolled back the stone and sat on it. His appearance was like lightning, and his clothes were white as snow. The guards were so afraid of him that they shook and became like dead men.

The angel said to the women, "Do not be afraid, for I know that you are looking for Jesus, who was crucified. He is not here; He has risen, just as He said."

Matthew 28:1-6 (NIV)

Abou Ben Adhem

Abou Ben Adhem
   (may his tribe increase!)
Awoke one night from a deep dream of peace,
And saw within the moonlight in his room,
Making it rich and like a lily in bloom,
An angel writing in a book of gold;
Exceeding peace had made Ben Adhem bold,
And to the Presence in the room he said,
"What writest thou?" The vision
   raised its head,
And with a look made of all sweet accord,
Answered, "The names of those
   who love the Lord."
"And is mine one?" said Abou.
   "Nay, not so,"
Replied the angel. Abou spoke more low,
But cheerily still, and said
   "I pray thee, then,
Write me as one that loves his fellow-men."
The angel wrote, and vanished.
   The next night
It came again, with a great wakening light,
And showed the names whom love
   of God had blessed;
And, lo! Ben Adhem's name led all the rest!

—Leigh Hunt

Archangel Gabriel From: Polyptych of the Mystic Lamb, 1426
Jan van Eyck, c. 1390-1441, Flemish   St. Bavon Cathedral, Ghent

DARK ANGELS

All God's angels come to us disguised;
Sorrow and sickness, poverty and death,
One after another lift
    their frowning masks,
And we behold the Seraph's face beneath,
All radiant with the glory and the calm
Of having looked upon the front of God.

          —James Russell Lowell

Life is so generous a giver, but we,
Judging its gifts by their covering,
Cast them away as ugly, or heavy,
    or hard.
Remove the covering, and you will find
    beneath it
A living splendor, woven of love,
    by wisdom, with power.
Welcome it, grasp it, and you touch the
Angel's hand that brings it to you.
Everything we call a trial, a sorrow,
    or a duty,
Believe me, that Angel's hand is there.

          —Fra Giovanni

Azrael

The angels in high places
Who minister to us,
Reflect God's smile, their faces
Are luminous;
Save one, whose face is hidden,
(The Prophet saith).
The unwelcome, the unbidden,
Azrael, Angel of Death.
And yet that veilèd face, I know
Is lit with pitying eyes,
Like those faint stars, the first to glow
Through cloudy winter skies.

That they may never tire,
Angels, by God's decree,
Bear wings of snow and fire—
Passion and purity;
Save one, all unavailing,
(The Prophet saith),
His wings are gray and trailing,
Azrael, Angel of Death.
And yet the souls that Azrael brings
Across the dark and cold,
Look up beneath those folded wings,
And find them lined with gold.

—*Robert Gilbert Walsh*

Angel Musicians, Detail
from the Vallombrosa Altar

Pietro Vannucci Perugino, c. 1445-1523
Italian, Galleria dell'Academia, Florence

The Fall of Lucifer

The All-Powerful had
Angel-tribes,
Through might of hand,
The holy Lord,
Ten established,
In whom He trusted well
That they His service
Would follow,
Work His will;
Therefore He gave them wit,
And shaped them with His hands,
The holy Lord.
One He had made so powerful,
So mighty in His mind's thought,
He let him sway over so much,
Highest after Himself
    in Heaven's kingdom.
He had made him so fair,
So beauteous was his form
    in Heaven,
That came to him from the Lord
    of hosts,
He was like to the light stars.

Dear was he to our Lord,
But it might not be hidden from Him
That His angel began
To be presumptuous . . .
Then was the Mighty angry;
The highest Ruler of Heaven
Hurled him from the lofty seat;
Hate had he gained of his Lord,
His favor he had lost . . .
The fiend with all his comrades
Fell then from Heaven above,
Through as long as three nights
    and days,
The angels from Heaven into Hell;
And them all the Lord transformed
    to devils,
Because they His deed and word
Would not revere . . .

For their sinful course
He filled Hell
With the apostates.

—*Caedmon*

War in Heaven

And there was war in heaven.
Michael and his angels fought
against the dragon, and the
dragon and his angels fought
back. But he was not strong
enough, and they lost their place
in heaven. The great dragon was
hurled down—that ancient ser-
pent called the devil or Satan,
who leads the whole world
astray. He was hurled to the
earth, and his angels with him.

Revelation 12:7-9 (NIV)

Detail of Heaven from *The Last Judgement*
Fra Angelico
c. 1387-1455, Italian
Museo di San Marco dell'Angelico, Florence

The Four Angels

After this I saw four angels standing
at the four corners of the earth, hold-
ing back the four winds of the earth
to prevent any wind from blowing on
the land or on the sea or on any tree.
Then I saw another angel coming up
from the east, having the seal of the
living God. He called out in a loud
voice to the four angels who had
been given power to harm the land
and the sea: "Do not harm the land
or the sea or the trees until we put a
seal on the foreheads of the servants
of our God."

Revelation 7:1-3 (NIV)

The Seven Angels

And I saw the seven angels who stand before God, and to them were given seven trumpets.

Another angel, who had a golden censer, came and stood at the altar. He was given much incense to offer, with the prayers of all the saints, on the golden altar before the throne. The smoke of the incense, together with the prayers of the saints, went up before God from the angel's hand. Then the angel took the censer, filled it with fire from the altar, and hurled it on the earth; and there came peals of thunder, rumblings, flashes of lightning and an earthquake.

Then the seven angels who had the seven trumpets prepared to sound them.

Revelation 8:2-6 (NIV)

The seventh angel sounded his trumpet, and there were loud voices in heaven, which said: "The kingdom of the world has become the kingdom of our Lord and of His Christ, and He will reign forever and ever."

Revelation 11:15 (NIV)